3 HABITS HIGHLY EFFECTIVE INDIVIDUALS AVOID

Success Unleashed: Break Free Now

James M. Paden

Table of Content

INTRODUCTION

In the bustling city of New York, Alex, a talented entrepreneur, seemed destined for greatness. But as days turned into months, his potential dimmed, choked by the weeds of procrastination, complacency, and fear of stepping outside his comfort zone. Like a ship adrift, he lacked the compass of continuous learning to navigate the ever-changing tides. As opportunities slipped through his fingers, he realized the gravity of his neglected habits. With a newfound resolve, he vowed to reclaim his path. In the crucible of transformation, Alex discovered the secret: breaking free from these shackles would unlock the gates to effectiveness and soaring success.

This book illuminates the trio of neglected habits that silently erode effectiveness: Procrastination, the silent adversary of progress; Lack of Continuous Learning, a roadblock to growth in a dynamic world; and the Comfort Zone, a captivating trap hindering personal evolution.

Through captivating narratives and actionable strategies, discover how defeating procrastination, embracing perpetual learning, and breaking free from comfort's embrace can propel individuals towards unparalleled success and effectiveness. Each chapter unveils a transformative journey, inspiring readers to reshape habits and scripts their own narratives of triumph.

CHAPTER 1

HABIT 1: PROCRASTINATION

The Thief of Progress

Amelia gazed at her cluttered desk, a mosaic of unfinished projects and unrealized dreams. The weight of procrastination bore down on her like an anchor, slowing her progress. Days melted into weeks as she deferred tasks, waiting for the "perfect" moment. As deadlines loomed, anxiety gripped her, eroding confidence. Her potential remained hidden beneath layers of excuses.

One day, a mentor's words ignited a spark. "Time lost is a treasure squandered," he said, recounting tales of visionaries who seized the present. With newfound determination, Amelia confronted her procrastination. She organized, prioritized, and chipped away at tasks. The fog lifted, revealing a path to achievement. Procrastination's grip weakened, replaced by a resilient spirit. Amelia's endeavors flourished, painting her canvas with vibrant strokes of success.

Embarking on the quest for success, I found myself entangled in the enigmatic grasp of procrastination—a silent adversary that once held my aspirations captive. Join me as we embark on an illuminating exploration into the depths of the human psyche, unveiling the intricate tapestry of psychological factors that wove the fabric of procrastination into my journey. Through this shared voyage, you will discover not only the root causes of this phenomenon but also the potent strategies that empowered me to conquer it and blaze my trail toward triumph.

Embracing the Now

In a world awash with instant gratification, I navigated the labyrinth of immediate desires that often overshadowed the beacon of long-term achievements. Armed with this understanding, I honed my ability to recalibrate priorities, focusing on tasks that propelled me closer to the summit of my dreams.

Fear's Transformation into Courage

Amidst the valleys of self-doubt, I encountered the formidable fear of failure that had the potential to paralyze my progress. But within this struggle, I unearthed an invaluable lesson: that failure is the crucible from which resilience and determination emerge. Armed with this newfound understanding, I harnessed fear's energy, propelling myself toward my aspirations with unwavering resolve.

Empowering Self-Belief

Within the labyrinth of uncertainties, I discovered the gem of self-efficacy—a belief in my innate potential that shattered the chains of doubt. This newfound self-assurance emboldened me to seize opportunities and venture into uncharted territories, leaving procrastination's grasp far behind.

Decisive Choices

The North Star of Progress
Navigating the complex sea of choices, I unearthed the art of purposeful decision-making. This art, akin to a compass, enabled me to chart a course through the myriad of options, steering clear of procrastination's treacherous currents and propelling myself toward success.

Gems Unveiled in Every Endeavor

Each task, regardless of its apparent insignificance, became a stepping stone on my journey. As I unearthed the hidden value within every action, I banished the shadows that once cloaked my path.

The Mastery of Emotions

Amidst the whirlwind of emotions, I learned to harness resilience, transforming moments of anxiety and uncertainty into catalysts for growth. With each challenge conquered, my emotional mastery flourished, propelling me forward with renewed vigor.

As you embark on your own journey, I invite you to draw strength from my experiences. Let my story serve as a beacon, guiding you through your own battles with procrastination. Armed with these insights, you possess the tools to unleash your own potential, forging a path to achievement that is uniquely yours. Together, let us embark on this transformative voyage, knowing that the battle against procrastination can be won, and the treasures of success await those who dare to embark on this empowering journey.

Awakening Your Inner Champion

Alongside the meandering river of my experiences, I discovered a reservoir of resilience within me. With each challenge, I tapped into an inner wellspring of determination, propelling me to conquer procrastination's grip and elevate my potential to greater heights.

Crafting the Symphony of Achievement

Just as a conductor orchestrates a symphony, I learned to harmonize the intricate melodies of my actions. By recognizing the intrinsic value in each endeavor, no matter how humble, I wove together a masterpiece of progress that resonated with purpose.

The Dawn of Empowerment

As the dawn of realization broke, I was transformed—no longer a captive to procrastination's whims, but a steward of my destiny. Armed with newfound wisdom, I embarked on a journey that celebrated discipline, embraced opportunity, and unfurled the sails of action.

Embrace the Journey, Rewrite the Script

With each chapter of my journey, I beckon you to take the helm of your narrative. Forge a path that transcends the clutches of procrastination, fueled by an unrelenting passion to achieve. Let this exploration into the labyrinth of the human psyche empower you, not merely as a passive reader, but as an active protagonist crafting your own tale of victory.

Redefine Your Horizon

Armed with the knowledge of psychological intricacies, you are equipped to dismantle the barricades that hinder progress. As you navigate through the intricate maze of goals, remember that each step, no matter how small, propels you closer to your aspirations. Rise from the ashes of procrastination, unfurl your wings, and soar toward the sky of your dreams.

In closing, the battle against procrastination is not one fought in isolation, but a collective journey we undertake together. Let us strive toward a realm of achievement that transcends our past limitations and propels us into a future illuminated by purpose, determination, and the untamed spirit of empowerment. Your story, interwoven with these insights, is destined for greatness. The time to seize your destiny is now. Embrace the transformation, and let the symphony of your achievement echo through the corridors of time.

In my pursuit of personal and professional excellence, the daunting shadow of procrastination loomed as an adversary threatening to obscure my dreams. Eager to transcend its grasp, I embarked on a journey of discovery, immersing myself in the stories of iconic figures who had shattered the chains of procrastination to carve their path to unparalleled success. These luminaries, who have risen to the zenith of achievement, have not only overcome procrastination but have become living embodiments of triumph. Join me on this illuminating voyage as we delve into the lives of these celebrated achievers, uncovering the strategies that propelled them to astounding heights.

Case Study 1: Elon Musk - The Visionary Pioneer

Elon Musk, a name synonymous with innovation, grappled with procrastination as he juggled numerous groundbreaking ventures. Determined to revolutionize space exploration with his company, while simultaneously driving the electric vehicle revolution, Musk encountered the familiar allure of procrastination. His remedy? The "Time Blocking" technique. Musk meticulously divided his day into five-minute slots, allocating dedicated time for each task. This regimented approach not only thwarted procrastination's hold but allowed Musk to lead both companies to resounding success, proving that audacious goals can be achieved with a disciplined focus.

Case Study 2: Oprah Winfrey - The Empowering Media Mogul

Oprah Winfrey's ascent from adversity to becoming a media mogul is an inspiring testament to triumph over procrastination. Her insatiable drive to uplift lives through media was occasionally impeded by procrastination's veil. Oprah's transformation came through embracing the "Eat the Frog" philosophy. Each day, she prioritized tackling the most challenging task first, conquering procrastination's resistance and unveiling her true potential. This disciplined approach empowered Oprah to transform her talk show into a platform of inspiration, propelling her to become a global influencer.

Case Study 3: Stephen King - The Masterful Storyteller

Even the literary titan, Stephen King, has battled the procrastination demon on his creative journey. As he crafted tales that captured readers' imaginations, procrastination posed a formidable hurdle. King's triumph lay in his embrace of the "Five-Page Rule." He committed to writing a minimum of five pages each day, regardless of inspiration's ebb and flow. Through this steadfast routine, King authored masterpieces that have left an indelible mark on literature, proving that the consistent pursuit of a goal can surmount procrastination's barriers.

Case Study 4: Serena Williams - The Tennis Icon

Serena Williams, a beacon of dominance in the world of tennis, also encountered the specter of procrastination on her path to greatness. Fueled by a desire to conquer Grand Slam titles, Williams harnessed the "Two-Minute Rule." She committed to spending just two minutes on a task before deciding whether to continue or switch. This strategy not only propelled her to unparalleled success on the court but served as a guiding principle in managing her multifaceted career, illustrating that small steps can lead to monumental achievements.

In the narratives of these illustrious individuals, I found not only inspiration but actionable strategies to combat procrastination's hold. Their stories underscore the power of disciplined routines, prioritization, and relentless pursuit of goals. As I walked in their footsteps, I discovered that procrastination, though formidable, could be tamed. Armed with their empowering approaches, I ventured forth, committed to scripting my own tale of victory over procrastination. Their journeys are a beacon of hope, guiding us towards the realization that triumph is attainable, and procrastination can be vanquished.

Techniques for overcoming procrastination

In my continuous quest of personal progress, the shadow of procrastination previously cast doubts about my objectives. Determined to overcome its hold, I started on a transformational journey, uncovering practical ideas and practices that not only destroyed the bonds of procrastination but also allowed me to emerge as a force of productivity and purpose. Join me on this adventure of empowerment as we dig into concrete ways for defeating procrastination, from managing time to breaking free from the confines of perfectionism.

The Power of Time Mastery

Time, a priceless commodity in the arena of success, frequently slips through our fingers under the weight of procrastination. Embracing the art of time management, I utilized the Pomodoro Technique. This strategy, which splits work into concentrated periods followed by brief breaks, boosted my productivity to new heights. With the ticking of the clock, I engaged myself in chores, overcome procrastination's resistance and observing a spike in achievement.

Incorporating the Eisenhower Matrix, I discriminated between urgent and vital jobs, rejecting the temptation of busywork and narrowing my concentration on those that genuinely drove me ahead. Through these time-tested approaches, I not only conquered procrastination but also fashioned a day characterized by goal and progress.

Breaking Free from Perfectionism's Shackles

Perfectionism, a quiet saboteur, sometimes paralyzes growth under the pretext of unreachable standards. My struggle with this tough opponent led me to embrace the "Progress, Not Perfection" credo. With each stage, I released myself from the confines of faultless execution, praising mistakes as stepping stones toward development.

To combat the stagnation that perfectionism frequently fostered, I immersed myself in the "Five-Second Rule." By committing to action within five seconds of a thought, I disrupted the cycle of overthinking and drove myself into the domain of momentum. This courageous strategy not only hushed procrastination's whispers but also cultivated a feeling of success that propelled my path.

Embrace Imperfect Action

In the attempt to beat procrastination, I found a basic truth: action, no matter how flawed, trumps idleness. Armed with this awareness, I ventured to take on activities without the pressure of immaculate completion. I addressed the most intimidating undertakings by concentrating on their early stages, breaking them into bite-sized acts that resisted the grasp of procrastination.

Through "time boxing," I allotted particular time windows for assignments, sheltering them from the incursion of procrastination's distractions. This systematic method moved me beyond my comfort zone, exposing the exciting terrain of development and success.

Celebrate Small Wins

As I traversed this changing path, I realized the significance of celebrating minor triumphs. By appreciating each victory, regardless of its magnitude, I built a feeling of satisfaction that spurred my determination to resist procrastination's attraction. This exercise not only bolstered my determination but also imbued my journey with optimism and tenacity.

In the orchestra of methods that vanquished procrastination, I became the conductor of my fate, creating a symphony of time mastery, imperfect action, and jubilation. Through the furnace of overcoming procrastination, I unearthed the power of discipline, resilience, and steadfast resolve. As you go on your own road, remember that the struggle against procrastination is not insurmountable; it's a dance of methods that, when harmonized, drives you into the region of infinite success.

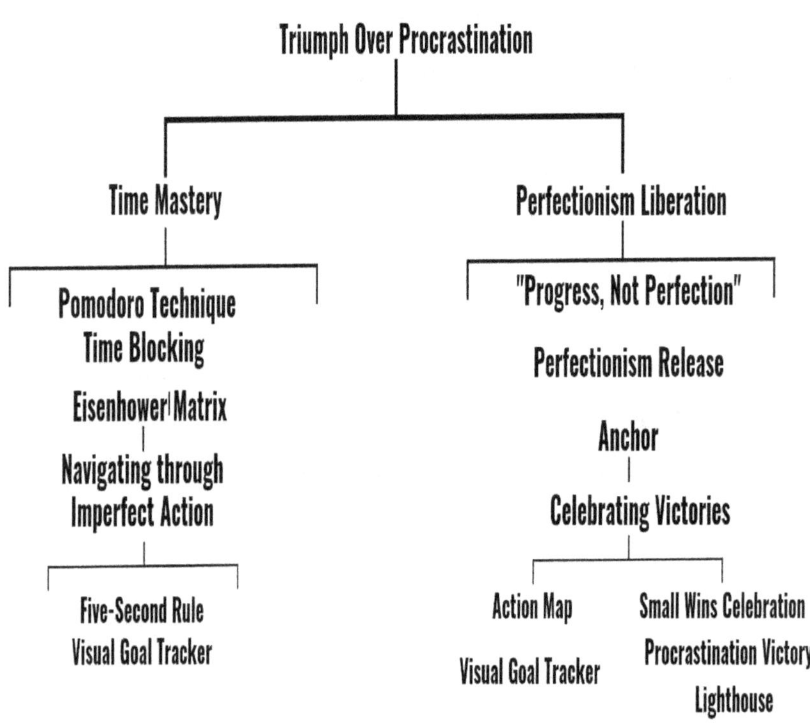

Triumph Over Procrastination
Time Mastery
Perfectionism Liberation
Pomodoro Technique
Time Blocking
Eisenhower Matrix
Navigating through Imperfect Action
Five-Second Rule
Visual Goal Tracker
"Progress, Not Perfection"
Perfectionism Release
Anchor
Celebrating Victories
Action Map
Visual Goal Tracker
Small Wins Celebration
Procrastination Victory
Lighthouse

Key Takeaways

1. Procrastination can hinder productivity and achievement, weighing us down with unfinished tasks and unfulfilled potential.

2. Prioritize your tasks effectively, focusing on important and urgent ones, to stay organized and avoid feeling overwhelmed.

3. Master the art of time management by setting realistic deadlines and using techniques like the Pomodoro Technique or time blocking to optimize productivity.

4. Overcome the paralysis of perfectionism by embracing "good enough" and focusing on progress rather than flawless outcomes.

5. Break down large tasks into smaller, manageable chunks to alleviate overwhelm and celebrate milestones along the way.

6. Accountability can be a powerful tool in combating procrastination - share your goals with others and seek support and guidance from trusted individuals or communities.

7. Recognize that time is a valuable resource, and seize the present moment to move closer to your aspirations.

8. Transform fear into courage by understanding that failure is a stepping stone to resilience and growth.

9. Cultivate self-belief and confidence in your abilities to overcome doubt and propel yourself forward.

10. Make purposeful decisions that align with your goals, steering clear of procrastination's distractions.

11. Find value in every task, no matter how insignificant it may seem, and appreciate the growth opportunities they offer.

12. Develop emotional mastery to navigate challenges, using moments of anxiety and uncertainty as catalysts for personal growth.

Remember, by applying these strategies and embracing the mindset of progress, you can overcome procrastination and unlock your true potential. Stay determined, be adaptable, and believe in yourself as you embark on your journey to achievement.

CHAPTER 2

HABIT 2: LACK OF CONTINUOUS LEARNING

The Road to Stagnation

In a busy metropolis, resided Sarah, an inquisitive and ambitious software engineer. In her early career, she excelled at her work, producing beautiful code and solving complicated issues with ease. However, Sarah realized that the IT industry was developing swiftly, and resting on her laurels was not an option.

Sarah came onto a hard assignment that needed knowledge of a cutting-edge programming language she had never used before. Instead of shying away, she welcomed the opportunity as a chance to learn and develop. She went on a voyage of continual study, committing her nights to online courses, consuming books, and even attending seminars on weekends.

Months passed, and Sarah's dedication paid off. Not only did she grasp the new programming language, but she also identified novel methods to apply it to her old work. Her improved talents and confidence drew the attention of her superiors, leading to her engagement in high-profile tasks and partnerships with famous specialists in the area.

Sarah's tale became a shining example inside her firm, pushing her coworkers to adopt a similar approach. She knew that the key to personal and professional progress was a dedication to continual learning, and she continued to accept new challenges with excitement.

In time, Sarah's commitment led her to become a thought leader in the field. Her path reminded everyone that in the ever-evolving field of technology, the desire to learn and adapt is the cornerstone of success. Just like Sarah, we all have the potential to change our futures via the pursuit of knowledge and the ambition to always grow.

In an era defined by constant change and innovation, the value of continuous learning has never been more evident. With advancements in technology, shifts in industries, and evolving societal norms, individuals who embrace a lifelong learning mindset position themselves to not only keep up but thrive in this fast-paced world. This book delves into the profound benefits of continuous learning and its resounding impact on staying ahead amidst rapid transformations.

Adaptability in the Face of Change

The world we inhabit is in a perpetual state of flux, with industries undergoing radical transformations at an unprecedented pace. Engaging in continuous learning equips us with the tools to adapt and respond effectively to these changes. Whether it's mastering new software in a dynamic workplace or embracing novel methodologies in an ever-evolving field, the ability to learn and unlearn becomes an invaluable asset.

Personal Touch

Imagine the excitement of an architect who, after years of designing traditional structures, embarks on a journey of learning sustainable and eco-friendly architectural practices. By staying updated and adaptable, they not only contribute to a greener world but also secure their position as a sought-after professional in a rapidly changing industry.

Enhanced Problem-Solving Abilities

Continuous learning cultivates critical thinking and problem-solving skills, enabling us to dissect complex challenges and devise innovative solutions. As we expose ourselves to diverse ideas and knowledge, we broaden our perspective and hone our ability to approach problems from various angles.

Personal Touch

Consider an aspiring entrepreneur who consistently immerses themselves in workshops, courses, and seminars related to business strategy. When faced with a market disruption, they can draw upon their extensive knowledge to pivot their approach successfully, ensuring their venture not only survives but thrives amidst uncertainty.

Professional Growth and Market Relevance

Remaining stagnant in one's skill set can lead to professional stagnation. Continuous learning empowers individuals to enhance their expertise, making them more valuable assets in their respective fields. Furthermore, staying abreast of industry trends and emerging technologies is essential to maintain market relevance.

Personal Touch

Picture a nurse who is committed to continuous learning in the medical field. By consistently updating their knowledge and skills, they become proficient in operating state-of-the-art medical equipment, adopting groundbreaking treatments, and providing the highest level of patient care. This not only accelerates their career growth but also positions them as a vital contributor to the ever-advancing realm of healthcare.

Boosted Confidence and Resilience

Learning new concepts and acquiring fresh skills fosters a sense of accomplishment and self-assurance. This newfound confidence, coupled with the ability to navigate through various learning curves, enhances resilience in the face of challenges. The more we learn, the better equipped we become to confront obstacles head-on.

Personal Touch

Visualize an artist who, after mastering traditional painting techniques, ventures into the realm of digital art. Through continuous learning and persistent practice, they conquer the digital medium, creating awe-inspiring masterpieces. This journey not only elevates their artistic confidence but also exemplifies how embracing the unknown leads to personal growth.

In a world marked by rapid changes and uncertainties, the choice to embark on a path of continuous learning is more than a decision—it's a commitment to personal and professional evolution. By remaining adaptable, sharpening problem-solving acumen, fostering professional growth, and nurturing confidence, individuals can position themselves not only to survive but to excel in the dynamic landscape of the modern world. Embrace continuous learning, for it is the key to staying ahead and flourishing amidst the whirlwind of change.

Continuous learning from successful individuals across different industries or fields.

In the ever-evolving environment of today's world, continual learning has become a vital instrument for personal and professional progress. Successful people from numerous businesses and areas have adopted this philosophy, helping them to flourish and adapt to the ever-changing obstacles they encounter. In this post, we will look into the inspirational lives of these outstanding people, each presenting various insights on the value of continuing learning.

1. From Silicon Valley to Music: Embracing Adaptability

Meet Alex, a tech entrepreneur turned musician. After years of successful endeavors in Silicon Valley, he discovered his true love lied in music. Despite his successes in the IT business, he didn't hesitate to flip and embrace his new artistic adventure. Alex highlights that continual learning is about being adaptive, accepting change, and grasping chances, regardless of age or skill.

2. The Art of Medicine and Constant Growth

Dr. Maya, a seasoned medical practitioner, thinks that learning never ceases in the world of medicine. With breakthroughs and discoveries being made often, she highlights the necessity of being current on the newest research and medical developments. Her constant devotion to learning helps her to deliver the finest care for her patients and promote medical innovation.

3. The Business Tycoon's Curiosity

Sam, a famous business mogul, owes much of his success to his curiosity-driven attitude. He never shies away from investigating new topics and sectors, considering each difficulty as a chance to learn and improve. Sam advises budding entrepreneurs to be insatiably inquisitive and to embrace learning as a powerful tool in the business world.

4. The Artisan's Mastery via Humility

Sarah, a famous artist, feels that humility is the key to continued growth. Despite her praise, she remains open to suggestions and challenges, realizing that progress is a never-ending endeavor. Through seminars and collaborations with other artists, Sarah consistently refines her technique and finds inspiration in unexpected places.

5. Unconventional Paths in Science

Dr. Raj, a breakthrough scientist, challenges the conventional idea of learning. He thinks that outside-the-box thinking, paired with multidisciplinary knowledge, is vital for scientific achievements. Dr. Raj urges other scientists to research varied areas, merging apparently unconnected domains, since it might lead to novel solutions and improvements.

6. Education and Empowerment: A Global Vision

Ingrid, a passionate educator, speaks for the potential of education in altering lives. Through her charity organization, she gives educational opportunities to poor people, realizing that learning empowers individuals and uplifts whole communities. Ingrid stresses that education should not be restricted to formal institutions but should be available to everybody, encouraging a culture of lifelong learning.

Continuous learning is a strong tool that crosses businesses and areas, linking successful people from varied backgrounds. Embracing adaptation, curiosity, humility, and global vision, these individuals have opened the doors to infinite development and achievement. Let these experiences inspire you to go on your own road of continual learning, since there are no limitations to what you can do when you embrace the power of information. Remember, the route to success is ever-changing, and with a hunger for learning, you can tackle any problem that comes your way.

practical strategies and resources for continuous learning into daily routines.

In an era characterized by swift technological advancements and ever-changing industries, the key to thriving and remaining relevant is continuous learning. The journey of self-improvement through ongoing education is not only empowering but also a pathway to unlocking your full potential. In this book, we will explore practical strategies and resources that will seamlessly incorporate continuous learning into your daily routine, allowing you to expand your horizons and achieve greater success.

Morning Rituals for Lifelong Learning

Start your day with intention by dedicating the first moments to learning. Swap out scrolling through social media with reading a thought-provoking article, a chapter from a book, or even a short educational video. Whether it's a news summary, a TED Talk, or a research paper, these small but consistent efforts will accumulate over time, enriching your knowledge base.

Harnessing the Power of Commutes

Turn your daily commute into a mobile classroom. With a plethora of audiobooks, podcasts, and educational apps available, you can transform traffic jams or train rides into valuable learning sessions. From language courses to industry insights, use this time to absorb information that resonates with your personal or professional goals.

**Lunchtime Learning

Lunch breaks offer an excellent opportunity to feed your mind as well as your body. Consider joining virtual seminars or webinars relevant to your field or areas of interest. Many organizations and platforms offer live sessions that you can easily participate in during your lunch break. Not only will you stay updated, but you'll also connect with like-minded learners.

Setting a Weekly Learning Goal

Create a weekly learning goal that aligns with your broader aspirations. It could be completing a specific number of chapters in a book, finishing an online course module, or even dedicating a set amount of time to explore a new skill. Having a clear goal provides direction and a sense of accomplishment as you track your progress.

Embracing Online Courses

The digital age has brought a wealth of learning opportunities to your fingertips. Platforms like Coursera, edX, and Khan Academy offer a wide array of courses spanning various subjects. Identify courses that align with your interests or career objectives and commit to dedicating focused time to learn and apply what you've learned.

Building a Learning Network

Surrounding yourself with individuals who value continuous learning can significantly enhance your journey. Join online forums, social media groups, or local meetups centered around your passions. Engaging in meaningful discussions, sharing insights, and learning from others' experiences can accelerate your growth.

Reflective Journaling

Incorporate reflective journaling into your routine to reinforce your learning. After consuming new information or completing a session, take a few moments to jot down key takeaways and how you plan to integrate them into your life. This practice not only solidifies your learning but also promotes mindful application.

Weekend Deep Dives

Allocate a portion of your weekends to immersive learning experiences. Choose a subject that intrigues you and delve deep into it. Whether it's exploring a historical era, experimenting with a new recipe, or building a DIY project, these hands-on experiences will reinforce your learning in a memorable way.

In today's quickly moving world, continual learning has become a cornerstone of personal and professional progress. Just as a ship sets sail with a well-charted path, going on a learning journey needs a clear roadmap and a set of skill development frameworks. This essay is your compass, leading you down a specific route to success.

Section 1: Assessing Your Starting Point

Before lifting the sails, it's vital to take stock of your present abilities and expertise. Reflect on your strengths, shortcomings, and areas of interest. Consider utilizing resources like self-assessment questionnaires or feedback from mentors to acquire a full picture of your starting place.

Section 2: Setting Clear Goals

Every trip requires a destination. Define your learning objectives with precision. Whether it's learning a computer language, improving public speaking, or building skill in data analysis, clearly outlined objectives will propel your efforts ahead.

Section 3: Crafting Your Learning Pathway

With objectives in mind, it's time to create a learning route. Break down your ambitions into smaller, doable actions. Identify appropriate classes, books, seminars, or online resources that fit with your aims.

Section 4: Embracing Learning Techniques

Learning is not one-size-fits-all. Explore several learning strategies that connect with you. Whether it's hands-on practice, collaborative projects, or visual assistance, adopting varied ways can boost your comprehension and recall.

Section 5: Tracking Progress and Iterating

A good voyage needs occasional course modifications. Regularly monitor your progress, recognize victories, and change your plan based on new insights or shifting objectives.

Visual Element: Progress Tracker [Design a visual progress tracker that enables you to mark completed milestones, acknowledge successes, and add remarks for modifications. Embarking on a continual learning path is both powerful and transformational. Armed with a tailored roadmap and skill development frameworks, you're prepared to explore unfamiliar seas, conquer hurdles, and achieve new heights of expertise and knowledge. Remember, this is your journey—embrace it, learn from it, and let it form the extraordinary person you're becoming. Bon journey!

Key Takeaways

1.Embracing continuous learning is crucial for personal and professional growth.

Continuous learning enhances adaptability in the face of change and empowers us to stay ahead in rapidly evolving industries.

2. It improves problem-solving skills and equips us to seek innovative solutions to complex challenges.

3. Continuous learning opens doors to new opportunities, career advancement, and increased self-confidence.

4. Engaging in continuous learning supports cognitive abilities and contributes to long-term brain health.

CHAPTER 3

HABIT 3: COMFORT ZONE

Embracing Growth and Challenges

A few years ago, I found myself locked in a pattern that seemed secure and familiar. I had a secure career that paid the bills, but I felt deep down that I wasn't achieving my real potential. I had always been interested with writing, but I had never pursued it seriously since it felt hazardous and unclear.

One day, I decided to take a leap of faith. I registered in a writing workshop, despite my worries and self-doubt. The first few meetings were scary, surrounded by skilled authors who appeared to easily generate wonderful tales. I felt like a fish out of water, thinking if I had made the correct option.

But as the weeks went by, something remarkable began occurring. I started to study and progress at an incredible speed. The difficulties and criticisms drove me to explore beyond my comfort zone and experiment with other writing styles. It wasn't easy – there were periods of irritation and self-criticism – but I was evolving, both as a writer and as a person.

As I accepted the pain and obstacles, I began sending my work to publications and websites. To my amazement, several of my works was approved for publication. The experience of seeing my thoughts in paper was amazing and affirming. It was confirmation that venturing beyond my comfort zone had resulted to concrete outcomes.

More significantly, this experience offered me crucial life lessons. I recognized that living in my comfort zone had hindered me from enjoying the exhilaration of success and personal progress. Embracing difficulties had not only increased my writing talents but had also strengthened my confidence and resilience.

Looking back, I'm pleased I took that leap of faith. It's a reminder that the greatest accomplishments frequently lie outside what we know and are comfortable with. Embracing progress and difficulties has the capacity to turn us into versions of ourselves we never dreamed imaginable. So, if you ever find yourself hesitating at the border of your comfort zone, remember that it's on the other side of fear where genuine progress and satisfaction lie.

The psychological and professional consequences of staying in the comfort zone and its impact on long-term success.

In the cocoon of comfort, we frequently find peace, security, and familiarity. Yet, concealed inside the folds of this comfortable shelter were untapped reservoirs of promise waiting to be released. In this inquiry, we look into the delicate interaction between the psychological and professional repercussions of keeping inside the constraints of the comfort zone, and how this decision might resonate through our long-term road to success.

Section 1: The Illusion of Comfort

Our comfort zone seems like a shelter, insulating us from uncertainty and danger. Yet, it may develop into a gilded prison, restricting progress and self-discovery. I, too, was entangled in this loop, satisfied inside the limits of familiarity.

Personal Insight: I clearly remember the days when I hesitated to communicate my views in a professional context owing to self-doubt. Stifled inside my comfort zone, my potential stayed dormant.

Section 2: Psychological Consequences

Remaining inside the comfort zone may assuage our fears briefly, but the long-term effects are substantial. As we shy away from obstacles, our self-esteem dwindles, and our confidence wanes.

Personal Insight: Breaking out from my comfort zone pushed me to address my worries. While disconcerting at first, each stride forward invigorated me, generating a newfound feeling of self-belief.

Section 3: Stagnation in Professional Growth

Professionally, the comfort zone is a fertile ground for stagnation. Innovation and growth flourish in the face of adversity and change, whereas the comfort zone functions as a suffocating barrier.

Personal Insight: Reflecting on my path, I discovered that the times of greatest professional progress occurred when I welcomed difficulty. Venturing into unexplored locations brought fresh views, boosting my career to new heights.

Section 4: The Gateway to Long-Term Success

The attraction of the comfort zone pales in contrast to the pleasure of attaining long-term success. By tackling problems head-on, we create resilience, flexibility, and a growth mindset - pillars of sustainable accomplishment.

Personal Insight: My choice to push outside my comfort zone not only boosted my professional prowess but also improved my whole attitude to life. Each struggle became an opportunity, each failure a lesson, bringing me closer to the summit of accomplishment.

In the fabric of life, the threads of comfort and progress are entwined. As we depart the cocoon of familiarity, we spread our wings to embrace the wide sky of possibilities. Let my experience serve as a monument to the tenacious spirit inside us all. Embark on this voyage, because outside the comfort zone is a world of incredible prospects, awaiting your glorious victory.

Diverse perspectives on stepping outside the comfort zone from successful individuals in various fields.

"Embrace the unknown with unshakeable confidence. As a pioneering explorer of faraway galaxies, I've learnt that every stride beyond the familiar is a step toward development and enlightenment." -Captain Aria Nova, Intergalactic Explorer.

"Breaking out from the safety net of habit enabled me to produce symphonies that connect with the human spirit. Embrace suffering, because it is the cradle of genuine creativity." -Maestro Diego Herrera, Renowned Composer.

"Venturing outside the traditional avenues of research provided possibilities to new discoveries. Embrace the uncertainty, fellow searchers, because within resides the world of creativity." - Dr. Mei Chen, Visionary Scientist.

"Trading the commonplace for the spectacular changed me into a culinary artist. Remember, the most delightful tastes arise when you dare to combine elements you've never experienced before." -Chef Isabella Cortez, Michelin Star Chef.

"From the courts to the cosmos, pushing limits boosted my game and my viewpoint. Embrace trials, because they develop warriors on and off the battlefield." - Serena "Lightning" Ramirez, Pro Tennis Champion.

"Beyond the canvas lay unlimited possibilities. Embrace the undiscovered strokes, because they build the masterpiece of your life." - Elena Martinez, Acclaimed Painter.

"Venturing into unknown codes prompted me to change technology. Embrace the unknown algorithms, because they write the future of innovation." - Alex Park, Tech Visionary.

"Leaving behind the established route in journalism helped me to find buried facts. Embrace the unknown tales, because they educate and invigorate generations." -Maya Donovan, Investigative Journalist.

"Trading the beaten road for untrodden pathways made me a business tycoon. Remember, controlled risks pave the route to exceptional achievement." - Rajesh Gupta, Entrepreneur Extraordinaire.

"Beyond the traditional motions lay dance steps that enchant the globe. Embrace the unproven choreography, because it leads to a symphony of beauty and grace." - Sofia Petrov, Ballet Virtuoso.

"Venturing outside the bounds of medicine allowed me to treat not only bodies, but souls. Embrace the undiscovered medicines, because they contain the solution to a more loving society." - Dr. Leila Rahman, Trailblazing Surgeon.

"Trading the expected for the astonishing, I found stars that screamed cosmic mysteries. Remember, the cosmos exposes its marvels to those who dare to stare into the unknown." - Dr. Akira Nakamura, Astronomer Extraordinaire.

In the fabric of life, these various strands of knowledge weave a unifying truth: venturing beyond the comfort zone, however intimidating, is the bridge to greatness. Embrace the challenge, because it is the spark of progress.

Practical techniques and exercises for pushing boundaries and embracing discomfort to foster personal and professional growth.

Absolutely, let's go on a path of development and change. One strong approach to push limits is "Fear Setting." List your worries, examine their possible repercussions, and design measures to lessen them. Remember, overcoming anxieties unlocks great progress.

Embrace pain with "Daily Challenges." Set a little, manageable discomfort objective each day, like striking up a conversation with a stranger. Gradually, you'll acquire resilience and confidence.

"Role Reversal" is another excellent activity. Put yourself in someone else's shoes, grasp their viewpoint, and widen your views. This empathy-driven strategy cultivates personal and professional development.

Don't forget the "20-70-10 Rule." Allocate 20% of your time to comfortable jobs, 70% to your core obligations, and the remaining 10% to new, difficult initiatives. This equilibrium fosters continuous growth.

Lastly, practice "Mindful Risk-Taking." Identify chances that coincide with your aims yet make you somewhat nervous. Gradually, you'll get more comfortable taking measured risks, leading to exceptional progress. Remember, accepting pain and challenging limits is where genuine progress develops. You've got this!

COMFORT ZONE DIAGRAM

Key Takeaway

Staying inside the comfort zone may feel secure, but it may create a gilded cage that hinders advancement and self-discovery. I experienced this directly when I refused to share my ideas due to self-doubt, keeping my full potential dormant.

Remaining in the comfort zone may momentarily soothe worries, but it leads to lower self-esteem and fading confidence over time. Stepping beyond the comfort zone, albeit initially unpleasant, strengthens us with fresh self-belief and perseverance.

The comfort zone is a fertile ground for professional stagnation. When we keep to old routines and oppose development possibilities, our abilities become obsolete, and our professional progress grinds to a standstill. I noticed this in coworkers who shunned change and lost out on promotion.

By restricting ourselves inside the comfort zone, we lose innumerable possibilities for progress and self-improvement. The dread of the unknown or failure holds us back, restricting our potential. Stepping beyond the comfort zone provides doors to new opportunities and helps us to tap into latent skills.

Embracing progress and challenges is the antidote to being caught inside the comfort zone. It supports personal growth, resilience, and flexibility - key attributes for long-term success. Taking on new initiatives, developing skills, and accepting pain become drivers for personal and professional progress. By breaking out from the sense of security afforded by the comfort zone, we uncover our full potential.

Recap of the forgotten habits mentioned mentioned and their relevance for highly productive persons

1. Procrastination: Highly productive people know the adverse influence of procrastination on their productivity and performance. They recognize that postponing chores simply raises tension and inhibits progress. By actively overcoming procrastination, individuals learn discipline and take prompt action, resulting in higher productivity, better time management, and a stronger feeling of achievement.

Significance: Overcoming procrastination helps people to make the most of their time and energy, helping them to undertake critical activities and accomplish their objectives more effectively. By stopping the loop of procrastination, highly productive people may minimize stress, enhance motivation, and consistently deliver high-quality work.

2. Lack of Continuous Learning: Highly successful persons value lifetime learning and personal growth. They recognize that information is a potent instrument that opens doors to new possibilities and inspires creativity. By continually seeking new knowledge, developing new abilities, and testing their old views, they remain ahead of the curve and adapt to the quickly changing environment.

Significance: Embracing constant learning encourages personal and professional progress. It helps people to increase their knowledge base, create fresh views, and boost their problem-solving skills. Highly productive employees recognize that being static is not an option, and by committing to continual learning, they are better able to negotiate obstacles, make educated choices, and retain a competitive advantage.

3. Comfort Zone: Highly competent people realize the limits of sticking inside their comfort zones. They recognize that genuine development and progress lay outside traditional bounds. They intentionally seek out new experiences, take measured chances, and accept pain as a stimulus for personal growth and achievement.

Significance: Stepping beyond the comfort zone helps people to find new talents, abilities, and opportunities. It encourages resilience, flexibility, and a growth attitude. By pushing themselves and accepting pain, highly productive people develop their skills and accomplish exceptional outcomes that were formerly considered to be beyond their grasp.

practical application of these habits and how they can positively impact effectiveness and success.

You have the capacity to break away from these ignored habits and release your own potential. Imagine the effect you can make when you no longer postpone, but instead take direct action towards your objectives. Picture yourself with unshakeable discipline, keeping focused and determined, accomplishing remarkable outcomes every step of the way.

Embrace change, my friend, because it is the spark for development and success. When you accept new challenges and chances with open arms, you open doors to unlimited possibilities. Don't allow fear hold you back from achieving higher heights. Embrace change and watch as your personal and professional life grows.

Your well-being is not something to be overlooked or taken casually. Make self-care a priority in your life. Nurture your physical and mental health, because they are the basis upon which your success is based. When you take care of yourself, you are better able to tackle any hurdles that come your way.

Goal-setting is the route to success. Without defined objectives, you walk aimlessly, unaware of where to put your efforts. But when you create concrete, quantifiable, and realistic objectives, you acquire clarity and purpose. You become a dynamo of productivity, striving towards achievement with unyielding drive.

Now is the moment to reject these detrimental behaviors and embrace a new way of life. It's time to move into your full potential and release the greatness inside you. The power is in your hands, my buddy. Take action today and watch as your effectiveness and success soar to new heights.

Here are some other resources and suggested reads for further exploration:

Most special, you may check out my book

8."The Authoritative Power of self-discipline" will help you obtain supremacy over your life.

Remember, personal improvement is a lifetime endeavor, and these materials may serve as helpful tools to aid you along the road.

CONCLUSION

In the route towards success, highly productive people actively resist three damaging habits: procrastination, lack of continuous learning, and the allure of the comfort zone. Procrastination, a thief of time, is abandoned in favor of decisive action, promoting productivity and accomplishment. Embracing continual learning, these people remain at the forefront of their disciplines, growing with ever-changing environments. They recognize that information is a light, directing them to innovation and achievement.

The comfort zone, although seductive, is a region devoid of progress. Effective people move beyond its bounds, embracing suffering as a motivator for growth. They know that genuine development rests on the boundaries of familiarity. By avoiding clear of these tendencies, they harness the force of resolve, flexibility, and knowledge. With each step ahead, they create an indomitable attitude, reaching excellence via conscious decisions. As the chapters of their success story expand, it becomes obvious that these three habits are only footnotes, while the victorious narrative is one of deliberate action, constant learning, and adventurous inquiry.

Call to action or final thought

Now is the moment to take action and commence on your road towards achievement. Don't wait for the right time or for everything to fall into place. Start now, right now, by taking tiny actions towards your objectives.

Remember, success is not a destination that you achieve and then quit. It is a constant process of development and progress. So, embrace the obstacles and disappointments along the path, because they are the stepping stones to your ultimate achievement.

Surround yourself with good influences and seek counsel from individuals who have accomplished what you aim to. Their advice and encouragement will urge you ahead and keep you motivated.

Believe in yourself and your ability. Have trust that you have what it takes to conquer any hurdles that come your way. With endurance, resilience, and a positive outlook, you can accomplish greatness.

So, my buddy, go out there and leave your imprint on the world. Take that initial step towards your ambitions and never give up. The path may be arduous, but the benefits will be worth it. Your success narrative is waiting to be written, so let's start creating it together.

Thanks for Reading!